NFL TEAM STORIES

THE STORY OF THE

NEW YORK JETS

By Jim Gigliotti

Kaleidoscope
Minneapolis, MN

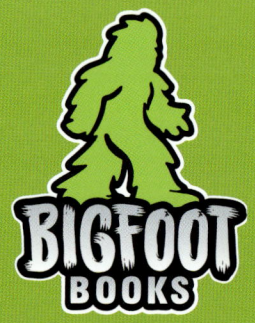

The Quest for Discovery Never Ends

· ·

This edition first published in 2021 by Kaleidoscope Publishing, Inc.

No part of this publication may be reproduced in whole or in part without written permission of the publisher.

For information regarding permission, write to
Kaleidoscope Publishing, Inc.
6012 Blue Circle Drive
Minnetonka, MN 55343

Library of Congress Control Number
2020936059

ISBN
978-1-64519-241-1 (library bound)
978-1-64519-309-8 (ebook)

Text copyright © 2021 by Kaleidoscope Publishing, Inc. All-Star Sports, Bigfoot Books, and associated logos are trademarks and/or registered trademarks of Kaleidoscope Publishing, Inc.

Printed in the United States of America.

FIND ME IF YOU CAN!

Bigfoot lurks within one of the images in this book. It's up to you to find him!

TABLE OF CONTENTS

Kickoff! **4**

Chapter 1: Jets History **6**

Chapter 2 Jets All-Time Greats **16**

Chapter 3: Jets Superstars **22**

Beyond the Book *28*

Research Ninja *29*

Further Resources *30*

Glossary *31*

Index *32*

Photo Credits *32*

About the Author *32*

KICKOFF!

"J-E-T-S!" New York Jets fans roar when their team takes the field.

"J!" they yell as loud as they can. . . "E!" . . . "T!" . . . "S!"

"J-E-T-S. Jets, Jets, Jets!"

Jets fans really care about their team. They have cheered for the team through good times and bad times. Unfortunately, there have been more bad times than good times. But the current Jets have an exciting young quarterback and some star players. Fans hope the good times are ready for takeoff again!

FUN FACT
The Jets share their home stadium with the New York Giants.

Waving green flags, Jets fans cheer on their team.

Chapter 1
Jets History

The Jets in action in 1965 in their green-and-white.

The Jets began play in 1960. At first, they were called the New York Titans. They were one of the original teams in the American Football League (AFL). The AFL teams joined the NFL in 1970. The Titans were called the Jets by that time.

The change came in 1963. The team wanted a name that sounded modern. Jet travel was still pretty new. So the team became the Jets. There was an added bonus. "Jets" rhymes with "Mets" and "Nets." Those are nicknames for New York teams in baseball and basketball! Jets fans also sometimes call their team "Gang Green." The team colors are green and white.

FUN FACT
AFL officials sometimes wore red-striped shirts!

The Jets began with a few down years. Then they became one of the AFL's best teams. The change started in 1965. The Jets **drafted** quarterback Joe Namath. He was a star at the University of Alabama. He soon began setting records in pro football.

Joe Namath

The Jets went to the Super Bowl after beating the Raiders.

Namath led the Jets to their first championship in 1968. The team beat the Oakland Raiders 27–23 for the AFL title. Then the Jets shocked the Baltimore Colts in the Super Bowl. The Colts were the NFL champions. But the Jets won 16–7. It is one of the most famous games in football history.

Jets fans would like to forget the 1970s. The team never had a **winning record** that decade! The 1980s were much better. The Jets made the playoffs four times in six seasons. The Jets set a club record by winning 12 games in 1998. They won their division for the first time. They made it to the AFC title game.

NEW YORK SACK EXCHANGE

The Jets featured one of football's best nicknames in the 1980s. The defensive line was called the New York Sack Exchange. The name was inspired by the New York Stock Exchange, a New York City landmark. The Sack Exchange helped the Jets win 10 games in 1981. They made the playoffs that year.

Defensive end Mark Gastineau

The Jets pulled off one of football's greatest **comebacks** in 2000. They beat the Miami Dolphins 40–37 in overtime. The game is called the "Monday Night Miracle." The Jets were losing 30–7. Then they scored 30 points in the fourth quarter.

That launched a good stretch for the team. The Jets won nine games that season. They made the playoffs six times in 10 years starting in 2001. They could not quite make it back to the Super Bowl, though.

Offensive lineman Jumbo Elliott made a key TD catch to beat the Dolphins.

The Jets haven't been to the playoffs since 2010. They have had a winning record only one time since then. It was in 2015. They won 10 games that year.

There is reason for hope, though. The team got off to a really bad start in 2019. Young quarterback Sam Darnold was sick early in the year. He got better. The team did, too! The Jets won six of their last eight games. The team can't wait to get back on the field in 2020!

QB Sam Darnold

It all starts with the center. The Jets signed Connor McGovern from the Broncos for 2020. He'll anchor the offensive line.

TIMELINE OF THE NEW YORK JETS

1960

1960: The Jets begin play in the AFL as the Titans.

1968

1968: The Jets win Super Bowl III.

1986

1986: The team makes the playoffs for the fourth time in six years.

1998

1998: The Jets win a club-record 12 games.

2010

2010: The Jets reach the AFC title game for the second year in a row.

2019

2019: The Jets go 6–2 in the second half of the season.

THE GUARANTEE

The Jets were expected to lose to the mighty Colts in Super Bowl III. It wasn't supposed to be close! Hardly anyone gave the AFL champs a shot. Jets quarterback Joe Namath had other ideas. "We're going to win," he told reporters. "I guarantee it."

The reporters did not think Namath was serious. Most athletes will not make such bold promises. But "Broadway Joe" really meant it. And he was right! The Jets won the game 16–7. They were clearly the better team that day. The offense was pretty good. Matt Snell ran for 121 yards and a touchdown. The defense was great. The Jets' Jim Turner kicked three field goals. Namath was the MVP . . . and backed up his guarantee!

Chapter 2
Jets All-Time Greats

Quarterback Joe Namath was the Jets' brightest star. He was popular on and off the field. He loved the New York spotlight. That's how he got his nickname of "Broadway Joe." Broadway is the name of a famous New York City street.

In 1967, Namath passed for 4,007 yards. That total was shocking. It was the first time a pro quarterback had ever reached 4,000 yards in a season. Lots of players have done it since. His total still remains the most ever by a Jets quarterback more than 50 years later! In 1985, Namath became the first Jets player to make the Hall of Fame.

FUN FACT
Namath led the league in passing yards three times.

Defensive end Mark Gastineau posted 22 sacks in 1984. He set an NFL single-season record. The mark stood until 2001. Gastineau and defensive tackle Joe Klecko were all-stars on the New York Sack Exchange.

Gastineau on the attack!

Mo Lewis

Shaun Ellis was a big-play defensive end for the Jets in the 2000s. He trails only Gastineau on the team's all-time sacks list. Maybe the best all-around defensive player in Jets history was linebacker Mo Lewis. He played in 200 games over 13 years starting in 1991. He was a sure tackler. He could rush the passer, too. Lewis made the **Pro Bowl** three times.

The Jets drafted running back Freeman McNeil number three overall in 1981. He led the NFL in rushing the next year. He was an all-star three times. McNeil set several club records. Curtis Martin came along to break them! Martin ran for more than 1,000 yards seven years in a row. He was elected to the Hall of Fame.

Don Maynard and Wayne Chrebet are the top two receivers in Jets history. Maynard played for the first Titans team in 1960. He retired in 1973. At that time, he had caught more passes than any other player! Chrebet played for the Jets from 1995–2005. He grew up not far from where the team plays its home games. He wasn't big or speedy. He just got the job done. Jets fans loved him!

Curtis Martin

JETS RECORDS

These players piled up the best stats in Jets history. The numbers are career records through the 2019 season.

Total TDs: Don Maynard, 88

TD Passes: Joe Namath, 170

Passing Yards: Joe Namath, 27,057

Rushing Yards: Curtis Martin, 10,302

Receptions: Don Maynard, 627

Points: Pat Leahy, 1,470

Sacks: Mark Gastineau, 74

Chapter 3
Jets Superstars

Today's Jets have pinned their hopes on quarterback Sam Darnold. He was only 20 when the team drafted him in the first round in 2018. He quickly became the team's starter. He was the youngest quarterback to start a game since the AFL teams joined the NFL in 1970.

Darnold passed for more TDs that year than any Jets rookie except Joe Namath. Late in 2019, he had his best game yet. He threw four TD passes, the most of his career. He also set a career passing yards mark with 293 yards. And best of all, the Jets won, beating Washington.

Jets fans want to see more games like that. The team believes Darnold has the special talent that all great quarterbacks have. He makes his teammates play better.

The Jets have given Darnold some good players to work with on offense. Le'Veon Bell can do it all at running back. He can catch the ball as well as he runs it. Bell starred for the Pittsburgh Steelers. Then he joined the Jets in 2019. He has made the Pro Bowl three times in his career.

Jamison Crowder turned into Darnold's best target in '19. He is a sure-handed receiver. Crowder caught 78 passes to lead the team. Ryan Griffin is a steady tight end. He had one of his best seasons in 2019. He caught a career-best five touchdown passes.

Tight end Ryan Griffin joined the Jets in 2019 after five seasons in Houston. His five TDs were second-best on the Jets.

Le'Veon Bell

Jamison Crowder

25

Jamal Adams

Rookie safety Jamal Adams did not make the Pro Bowl in 2017. "I won't miss another," he tweeted at the time. "Believe that." Jets fans believe! Adams has turned into one of the NFL's best defensive backs since then. And, yes, he made the Pro Bowl in the 2018 and '19 seasons.

Quinnen Williams is another young defender the Jets are counting on. He was the team's top draft pick in 2019. He is a huge presence in the middle of the defensive line. He is a force against the run. He can chase down the quarterback, too.

The Jets hope to fly high again for their fans. Let the chanting begin!

"J . . . E . . . T . . . S!"

Quinnen Williams

BEYOND THE BOOK

After reading the book, it's time to think about what you learned. Try the following exercises to jumpstart your ideas.

RESEARCH

FIND OUT MORE. Where would you go to find out more about your favorite NFL teams and players? Check out NFL.com, of course. Each team also has its own website. What other sports information sites can you find? See if you can find other cool facts about your favorite team.

CREATE

GET ARTISTIC. Each NFL team has a logo. The Jets logo shows the team name. Get some art materials and try designing your own Jets logo. Or create a new team and make a logo for it. What colors would you choose? How would you draw the mascot?

DISCOVER

GO DEEP! This book writes about the Jets' huge upset in Super Bowl III. Check out big upsets in other sports. What baseball or basketball or soccer teams won when they were not expected to? Who do you think was the biggest upset winner ever?

GROW

GET OUT AND PLAY! You don't need to be in the NFL to enjoy football. You just need a football and some friends. Play touch or tag football. Or you can hang cloth flags from your belt; grab the belt and make the "tackle." See who has the best arm to be quarterback. Who is the best receiver? Who can run the fastest? Time to play football!

RESEARCH NINJA

Visit **www.ninjaresearcher.com/2411** to learn how to take your research skills and book report writing to the next level!

RESEARCH

DIGITAL LITERACY TOOLS

SEARCH LIKE A PRO
Learn about how to use search engines to find useful websites.

FACT OR FAKE?
Discover how you can tell a trusted website from an untrustworthy resource.

TEXT DETECTIVE
Explore how to zero in on the information you need most.

SHOW YOUR WORK
Research responsibly— learn how to cite sources.

WRITE

GET TO THE POINT
Learn how to express your main ideas.

PLAN OF ATTACK
Learn prewriting exercises and create an outline.

DOWNLOADABLE REPORT FORMS

Further Resources

BOOKS

Jacobs, Greg. *The Everything Kids' Football Book (Sixth Edition)*. Avon, Mass.: Adams Media, 2018.

Morano Kjelle, Marylou. *Sam Darnold (Blue Banner Biographies)*. Hallandale, Fla.: Mitchell Lane Publishers, 2019.

Ryan, Todd. *New York Jets (Inside the NFL)*. Minneapolis, Minn.: Abdo Publishing, 2019.

WEBSITES

Factsurfer.com gives you a safe, fun way to find more information.

1. Go to www.factsurfer.com.
2. Enter "New York Jets" into the search box and click 🔍
3. Select your book cover to see a list of related websites.

Glossary

comebacks: defensive backs who cover an opponent's wide receivers. Cornerbacks make a lot of interceptions.

drafted: chosen in the NFL annual meeting that chooses players from college teams. Quinnen Williams was drafted by the Jets in the first round of the 2019 NFL Draft.

Pro Bowl: the NFL's annual all-star game. Jamal Adams made the Pro Bowl in 2020.

sack: a tackle of the quarterback behind the line of scrimmage. "The Sack Exchange" put a lot of QBs on the ground!

winning record: winning more games than losing. The Jets' last winning record came in 2015 when they were 10–6.

Index

Adams, Jamal, 26
American Football League (AFL), 7, 8, 9, 15, 22
Baltimore Colts, 9, 15
Bell, Le'Veon, 24
Chrebet, Wayne, 20
Crowder, Jamison, 24
Darnold, Sam, 12, 22, 24
Ellis, Shaun, 19
fans, 4, 10, 20, 22, 26, 27
"Gang Green," 7
Gastineau, Mark, 18, 19
Griffin, Ryan, 24
Klecko, Joe, 18
Lewis, Mo, 19
Martin, Curtis, 20
Maynard, Don, 20
McNeil, Freeman, 20
Miami Dolphins, 11
"Monday Night Miracle," 11
Namath, "Broadway" Joe, 8, 9, 15, 16, 22
New York Mets, 7
New York Nets, 7
New York Sack Exchange, 18
New York Titans, 7
Oakland Raiders, 9
Pittsburgh Steelers, 24
Snell, Matt, 15
Super Bowl, 9, 11, 15
University of Alabama, 8
Williams, Quinnen, 27

PHOTO CREDITS

The images in this book are reproduced through the courtesy of: AP Photos: 6, 8, 9; Al Messerschmidt 10, 11; Vernon Biever 14; NFL Photos 15, 18 ; Mitchell Reibel 16. Focus on Football: 12, 22, 24. Newscom: John Angelillo/UPI 4; Chris Williams/Icon SW 12; Lee K. Marriner/UPI 19; Anthony J. Causi/Icon SW 20; Joshua Sarner/Icon SW 24; Rich Graessle/Icon SW 25B, 27; Gregory Fisher/Icon SW 25T. **Cover:** Seth Wenig/AP.

About the Author

Jim Gigliotti was an editor at NFL Publishing for many years. Now he writes books for young readers.